Junction Road

JEAN HARRISON

Cinnamon Press
Independent Innovative International

Published by Cinnamon Press
Meirion House
Glan yr afon
Tanygrisiau
Blaenau Ffestiniog
Gwynedd
LL41 3SU
www.cinnamonpress.com

The right of Jean Harrison to be identified as author of this work has been asserted by her in accordance with the Copyright, Designs and Patent Act, 1988. Copyright © 2009 Jean Harrison
ISBN: 978-1-905614-81-3
British Library Cataloguing in Publication Data. A CIP record for this book can be obtained from the British Library.

Designed and typeset in Palatino by Cinnamon Press. Cover design by Mike Fortune-Wood from original Brick Wall by Ron Chapple Studios, agency dreamstime
Printed by MPG Biddles Ltd, Kings Lynn, Norfolk.

Acknowledgements:

Poems in this collection have previously been published in *Aireings, Dreamcatcher, Iota, Other Poetry, Rialto, The North, Seam, Smiths Knoll, Staple,* and the Cinnamon Press anthologies, *Sometimes, Wherever, Shape Sifting* and *Mint Sauce.*

Contents

to Barbara who has given hours listening and commenting.

Junction Road

Junction Road

Floorboards show through the carpet,
there's a bed where I've thrown my back-pack,
the view's fire-escapes and pigeons.

If I lean out I can see the way I came —
an alley where cement blocks lie at angles
like earthquaked stepping stones.

Before that I was waiting in the High Street
for a green man to show me across.
A girl in hijab avoided my eyes.

I crossed behind her in soft shoes,
my eyes on grey three-storey buildings,
unsure which one I wanted,

still hearing my mother, *Places like that*
are all right, if you've nowhere better,
and came to a lock where my key turned.

I'd packed my bag carefully,
one change of undies, unscented soap, one towel,
a note-book with a jazzy cover.

Blank

If I had a blank canvas in front of me
it would be so familiar:

side of a fridge
where I imagined polar bears;

fogged windows
Kent, Gloucestershire, Birmingham;

a face at the head of a table, air between us
like the torn sleeve of a school blouse;

starched napkins, white cloth,
empty wine-glasses like shadow policemen;

thin hair, a confused voice
asking questions it's too late to answer;

white enamel colander
I'd like to fill with water;

chalk cliff I might dare sketch now
with all its cracks and ledges.

The house on Frog Island

The car crosses no water
to reach a yard bounded by reeds
where father swings his black bag,
knocks on a white door, disappears.
What happens inside *Nothing to do with you.*

He's left her free
to stare at a wooden house
with one window, covered by a drawn curtain,
cast-iron down-pipe, row of seedy wallflowers,
beyond it, branches over a glinting river,

all so cut off the mill chimney can't spy in
to the shrunk flesh of ridged black planks
that keep him inside, upstairs in a sick-room
not looking out   *I want you*
exactly here when I come back.

She watches two Rhodes pecking the dust,
examines a peeling green water-butt
in a place that's only called an island,
draws a face on the dashboard, wonders
if she dare get out and feel the planks.

The bedroom

her chest-of-drawers between two windows
angled for the best light   rattly handles

when she opens the top drawers scent jerks out
in a puff of powder. *Lily-of-the-valley* she says
but it isn't like flowers.

boxes jars bags balls soft bundles
silk stockings she slides up white legs   as if for someone to see
next to them   folded   her knickers   her lacy petticoats

she's downstairs, using all the strength of a stringy arm
to poke the point of an iron into each corner of a pillow-case
grey hair wild across a cheek.

Right-hand top drawer, she said and I'm dithering
the chest's right—my left   but to try both   put my hand in
rummage for the hanky she wants   in front of a mirror

placed carefully across the corner
to show up smeared lipstick wrong colour of lipstick
wrong hand in the wrong drawer

look up into glass where light from two windows
shows two sides of a face don't match
but the eyes work together.

which is the true pair
those with their backs to my shoulder-blades
that see things the right way round   her in the kitchen

or these doubles   up here in her bedroom
staring back   reversed and tricky

Invader

I track the moon
right of the mullion, then left
not obviously moving,

always facing me
exploring the garden with radiant antennae
pouring in through the glass.

I don't want it in here
rolling around too bright to touch, alive
like the green numbers on the clock.

It will suck me in,
suck me dry, slide into my skin
and stare out.

Hilda

She lifts a wine-glass by the base,
turns it against the light, rubs with a soft cloth,
nearly midnight, guests all gone.

She searches for smudges, looking up
into a globe where the ceiling rotates,
the kitchen spins round her and carries the house with it:

lounge with re-plumped cushions, dining room
still smelling of food and blown out candles, a man
who insists he can't get to sleep without her.

The stem slides between her fingers
till the bowl rests in her palm,
she polishes again for total, see-through clarity,

pauses, the glass tilted against her life-line; raises it again,
way above her head at the end of its long stalk,
examines its outline against hard light.

Iona

This, she announces, *is the machair,*
and comes to a standstill
where the path disappears on grass
fringed with dry sea-weed.

There are no cows, though the dictionary
makes them essential *low-lying grass*
where cattle lie to chew the cud,
close to the sea.

They often spread their bellies on the sand
like seals — which aren't here today —
just a pair of eider and waves,
shushing over the pebbles.

Next stop America, and wind
strains her cagoule back towards land
as she faces into it, not exactly listening,
just staring at an empty beach

she last saw sixty years ago
a girl not normally a dreamer,
except once perhaps, when she migrated
south to England —

and there she has no use
for stories about wise women and singing seals,
calls them *over-romanticised bletherings*
of the Celtic Twilight.

She speaks her little bit of Gaelic
not for any magic
but in her careful, Lowland way
as the only term that denotes

exactly this place,
beside a ditch of yellow iris,
facing a sea where wind tugs white hair
loose from her bun.

Girl reading — *Picasso*

She's twisted sideways—a long nose
has found a book to get lost in—
on a table under a lamp

all of her in the one eye
which faces the viewer,
dominating her face.

She's not good-looking—
that's why she's not at a party or night-club—
they wouldn't know what to do with her—

and the book has drawn the rays of the lamp
down over her like a soft tent.
It's always been like that,

printed words always catching her,
pulling her aside, distorting her even,
though they've saved her too.

Christmas cactus

She hated its *bloodstained talons.*
Harpies, she said, thinking of women
who'd flourished cigarette-holders
with a dancer's sweep of the arm,
focussing

in a way she refused. She
ate books, not men.

Now she scans the same page over and over
because you must read
even if words perform ridiculous dances
and in the corner behind her a cactus
thrusts carmine tips out and over,

fireworks caught just before fadeout.

A look

You'll want to go up for a look.
So I went, not extra slowly,
up the wide dark stairs.
I'd never done this before.
I stood a little back from the bed,
looked diagonally
across sheets to the pillow,
gazed a little while,
walked to the window,
looked out at a Devon lane
in full mud under November trees;
returned to my place
to stand without thinking,
her face not being the same.

The study

She inspects the bureau. *You're not keeping it polished.*

I go on writing at her table in the middle of the room.
She used to keep it half-folded against the wall.
One arm of her sofa

appears on its own in front of the bureau.
She used to perch on it to write. Now she settles onto it,
rests her fingers on the corner of the flap, stares into the wood.

Sunshine fluffs the white hair over her double crown
and the corners of my skull firm up. The same shape.
Sometimes I'd like to take my head off.

The sofa pushes its back and cushions through my table,
scratches my knees with prickly nylon. Her fault it's here.
Didn't fetch much, I say, letting her know she doesn't count now.

And she is a little lighter. I feel I could move her round.
On her feet she firms up and roams the room
looking for things to re-arrange.

If I could control my head —
my eyes
force my wall up through her

and then she's solid again.
Your great-grandmother's bureau, she says.

Seeing blue

Last night our room overlooked a harbour
so close—marigolds in the window-box
glowed against slate-blue.

Boats were moored at the opposite jetty,
freshly painted, red, green, blue,
thin orange lines from a masthead light

vibrated on blue. I sat up in bed listening
to the whoosh of the shower and a towel rubbing
my head turned to look out.

In the night I peered under a black curtain,
at a pale sky, the sea lying there,
steel blue, faintly opalescent,

and knew my mother
grew up on another coast of the same sea.
Blue was her favourite colour.

She liked opals, and the sea is often
that mix of colours. Yesterday it was uniform,
subdued, without reflections.

In the morning a Galway Hooker shook out
two red sails, curved away round the pier
towards a line of blue humps and faded into the drizzle.

Tonight in another house I glance out at red and white cattle,
go to the bed, sit down, start arranging my things
and suddenly there's blue in front of my eyes.

War work

The catch on a window snibbed at nightfall
so downstairs shutters can be pulled up and bolted
against the prying eyes of planes;

the turn of the stairs where a child pauses,
just tall enough to see through banisters
to rattly glass behind thin black curtains,
the door of a room nearer a sky
she pictures full of flying faces;

and going back down she doesn't hold the rail
—it's a bit shaky—but looks over, tries to make sense
of black and white squares broken by table legs
in a hall where no voices carry through;

comes eventually to bread and butter
on plates painted with blue imaginary flowers,
a fire whose warmth goes mostly up the chimney,
two tired people in arm-chairs, the sound of chewing;
and chooses the heel

because teeth tugging on a leathery crust
are working at things.

Deposits

I've ducked under dim electric bulbs,
stared through grilles into backless passages,
a long way in under the mountain.

The guide switches off the lights;
space weighs in, light as the heart of a soap-bubble,
a waterfall haunts like an unexamined god.

Pale torch-light finds a row of grinning stalactites;
while he slips in *metamorphic, quaternary,*
we picture floods and volcanoes;

he names a tiny fern
lodged high up in the darkness,
enumerates species that left bones here

and I think about a Stone Age child
awake in an echoing labyrinth
while the family breathes round her.

At this time of morning

the garden's wearing ash and charcoal;
she couldn't say, *Because it's been burnt*;
—there are no jagged stumps.
 It's not mourning some lost perfection

just withdrawn, the topiaries chessmen
playing grandmother's footsteps,
hardly breathing
in a world the other side of glass.

A faint touch of biscuit is the fence
moving towards dawn,
two white flakes above it—
the pink rose—

—so there was a time
when pieris flamed with new leaves
gamboge iris nestled against the south wall,
maidenhair stuck green confetti over her trousers.

She stands at the window,
searches beyond black trees
for sun to call it all back,
or if not all, what is available today.

In that day

there'll be a house in red sandstone
among green hills
just gently
beginning to heave and stretch.

Early morning smoke
will puff a wavering speech bubble
across wobbling dry-stone walls,
mist will blur the valleys.

At this moment a man and three women
will be walking down a dim corridor
towards a chapel
an ancestor built out beyond the kitchens.

Outside, a car on an unseen road
will send a pheasant hurtling into the air
over a crack
where tower blocks are thrusting up.

The four will choose well separated seats,
break hesitantly into today's psalm:
How can we sing
the Lord's song in a strange land?

Why don't they look out of arched windows,
take in what hills are doing nowadays,
that the house
is alone and alien among them?

Instead they'll broaden into the Jubilate
O be joyful in the Lord,
though glancing sideways,
checking with one another how it sounds.

Education soon

Must have been strange
actually going to places. I try to imagine it.

I put on tactile gloves,
log onto the ground and it's trembling—
that's worms. I click a chatroom
speak to Teiko, Amma and Ming.
I've got the world for friends—Fatima,
Rosie, Mulinda, Oleg, Sundanatha and João.

You're not my teacher now, so here it is. Once
you'd given me bad marks for a really boring assignment
I clicked 'Undress' and you'd left your guard off...
Careless, weren't you? Mum thinks she's erased that ikon.

It wasn't what I'd expected
my eyes dropped and then
all by themselves went back and stared.

You were sitting and then you stood up
and went across to the bookcase, your clothes
like faint shadows around you, moving as you moved.
You took down a book and stood there with your first finger
laid along the spine, your body one smooth pathway
of curves and every part swayed gently
as you walked back to your seat.

So that's it, I thought, that's what it's like
when you're happy inside your skin,
I felt I'd arrived somewhere and now
I wanted to feel real air, walk up a hard street,
touch solid things.

High-wire

Dead cockroach, dusty smell, closed window,
silence where I can gather myself
for a view of the bush.

A line of pylons. A shrike
sways on a wire above tall grasses.
Four lions shoulder through.

Their glances travel a hundred yards of baked earth
and cut through glass. They drop their heads
with the strange shyness of cats

topaz eyes in triangular yellow faces,
the long, slow tugs of a lioness licking hr cubs
iron bars in the dark at the back of the Big Top,
shadowy figures dancing above them

and I remember
they shuffled back when Ted entered the cage,
jumped onto boxes and stared.

I open the door, stand in the porch
take deeper and deeper breaths
the only way—a straight line forward.

Abomination

We're just discussing why Saul
shouldn't have consulted the Witch of Endor
when they all rush to the window—down there
the school labourers are parading a dead python
that was lurking round dormitories, raising eyes out of drains,
preparing to unhook its lower jaw and swallow.

We'd love to hurtle down the echoing stairs,
out into sunlight between hibiscus hedges,
press together like a crowd round the Virgin,
slide the tips of our fingers over those cold scales;
the thickness of three waste-pipes tied together,
blue-grey back, whitish belly, on the shoulders of six men
strung out at three foot intervals,

a slitherer that stood on its tail in the Garden of Eden,
taught an Ashanti Adam and Eve to make love,
cuddled the new-made world, was fed by priests
in women's clothes, at Ouidah in return for oracles.

Habits

1

Little things sink in
like slipping off to St. Rose's Convent
to confer with another Head,

see a smile under a black wimple
watch hands gesture across a black skirt,
talk freely;

accept an invitation, descend past the chapel,
close her nose to the lingering scent of incense,
turn her eyes from holy water,

enter a nuns' parlour,
drink tea
under the Pope's photograph,

chat, listen, the talk extending and deepening
till she hears a text she hasn't heard before,
a non-Protestant birdsong.

2

Mist blurs mangoes and oil-palms,
the first buckets clank, girls call from the dormitories,
a bell-shrike tolls, a coucal pours a descending glug-glug-glug.

She sits by her bed, reads slowly, with prayer,
waits for things to clarify, a text to take on colour.
as they always have in quiet with a Bible,

lays the end of her contract
before the Lord
morning after morning

listening for a voice
that speaks to her through silence
not to be doubted—it brought her here—

At the far end of the compound
sun already touches scarlet hibiscus
edging a path between classrooms and front gate.

3

When things refuse to come clear
use your head, think,

you were right not to renew
right for a local to take over
you did right

(tell your heart to shut up, lie down,
padlock its lips)

write the big words—love etc
on billboards across the horizon

(your heart wants
what it has no right to want)

think about other people
consider the poor—displaced, shoved aside
lost in the inner city

go where you're needed,
where you understand the culture
go home

4

fold embroidered dresses
two from the old girls, one from friends
find a tea-chest for carved tables from the teachers
wind a sheet round a mosaic cockerel from the cooks
pile up cards, photographs

get them in the trunk
mustn't waste time
leave cushion covers and curtains
a set of crockery—James will take it—
set aside money for him to retire on
say good-bye to him—
he's old
and never learned to write

say good-bye to the bursar, the labourers,
the night-watchmen, townspeople,
the staff, one by one, coming up to the office
with personal gifts of cloth and polished deer

say good-bye.

5

And now

the street where she grew up
blocked off, without houses;
others with doors pierced
by star and crescent;

the skyline no longer
a rhythm of chimney-pots
the flat London sky
jagged with tower blocks;

A new vista
across the railway
to other-wordly, secular curves
of cooling towers;

Her cramped back room
lit only
by a view
down a narrow passage;

Her church
wire mesh across the windows,
her friends gazing out like netted fish,
hooked on the same old texts.

6

Four lime trees she passes every day
planted outside a London Board school,
Children bowled hoops round them.

Now the playground's protected by wire
and outside, roots heave up the asphalt,
Pedestrians trip over them.

7

She never sings at home
in that dark room
from which she can hardly see
her tiny garden
nor hear the thrush
that occasionally perches
on next door's shed.

In church
she throws back her head—
Watts, Wesley, Sankey and Moody,
Newton's *Amazing Grace,*

that she first heard from her office
as it flowed across the netball courts
from the spare flat in the staff quarters
where a missionary on holiday
was washing her undies

And when this heart and flesh shall fail

Again in London the last verse ripples up,
carries her to a heaven *bright shining as the sun.*

8

A friend shows her alien leaves
growing through a fuschia
says they're potatoes.
They prise out tubers

with threadlike necks
from twisting through roots,
swollen bellies that filled spaces,
weird enough for juju.

She lays them out on the ground,
picks them up, turns them over,
takes one indoors and plants it
casually on the mantelpiece

where it glowers from deep-set eyes. For days
she begs everyone who comes to the house
to tell her what it is, watches them
feel it too simple to say, *just a potato.*
It settles in, becomes dusty,

34

something that's there
when she stops discussing plans,
Our family don't make old bones.

9

Knots she falls over
pushed up by four dusty limes;

shadow from a brick wall
across a thin view from a back room;

hibiscus, bell-shrike,
girls calling over balconies;

old-fashioned hymns,
silent house;

advert she keeps inside her Bible
and reads over and over,

job in a convent school
she won't apply for;

lump growing in her stomach
nothing to bother about.

Sideways glance

The underground stretches out.
The air's been shut in a hundred years.
You're half-way down on a vandal proof bench

wearing African cloth. Printed vines
curl over your shoulders and cup your breasts,
your knees are apart, soles flat on the ground.

Lids curve over your eyes. Shadows
throw up your cheek bones. You're not asleep
just allowing carved lines to take you over.

I'd like to approach you and say, *Akwaaba,*
Welcome, letting my mouth fill
from the language your face brings back,

to hear its cadences once more in your reply,
just the odd word or two I understand
—we'd soon get back to English.

Your fingers dent a Heal's bag lightly.
A gold watch circles your wrist.
The indicator flickers,

your arms flow to your bags, you gather them
the way you'd order documents
or check an obstreperous grandchild,

dart a mischievous smile and slide away
towards daylight, some street, some house,
where people invest you in better fitting masks.

The breeze

Cool air breathes in, darkness thins
round dawning shapes, cupboards,
all open, displaying a hugger-mugger
assemblage of things

I owned once in other houses, or
have invented, had planted on me.
I'm waiting to find out
which doors could safely be closed.

What's the barometer doing on its head?
Why should anyone inflate a sock and seal it?
Was I the one twisted a crucifix into a corkscrew?
It's the angles that horrify. Who broke the mug

painted with scenes from Alice? Did she mean
to let loose the Jabberwocky? And the ring
in a heart-shaped box—did anyone wear it?
Did she love the giver?

In a far corner there's an oak tree painted on blue,
its reflection upside down in pink marble
as if a tree could grow again
from its own fossil.

The room swerves round me, elusive as a bat,
and when I reach out to a stone sill
it shifts in the breeze.

Woman on the moon

This is the longest night I've ever faced.
I'm putting it off while I write to you
watching blues creep up.

The earth has been huge in our sky all day
and as it sank, I felt I could reach out
and touch you, but all the time indigo
was seeping into the valley.
Now it's flooded and the hills
are like shadowed snow.

An hour ago we spoke by satellite.
You told me all you'd been doing.
I said I'd being X-raying moonrock
and you went quiet; that I'd been walking
and my footsteps would lie there always,
that there's no wind
and you said, *There must be.*

I said, *The light that comes here from earth*
is blue and I'm losing it. Nights here
are as long as fourteen days on earth,
and you said, *That doesn't make sense.*

It should soon be time for your father
to give you your supper and afterwards
both of you will go into the garden
but I'll be on the side of the moon
that's turning towards space.

Bindweed

We touched down bang on target,
half opened our helmets,
headed north to find the ruins.
Earth days flicked over us, day, night,
each gone in no time—so much shorter than ours

and the colours—just as the old people say,
not *changed by blue light from 'Home'*
—grass that was definitely green
more and more of it till we were wading
and found rubble draped with cheeky flowers.

We touched them and remembered Mother
staring into the long dark *The only light*
we get here is this ghostly reflection,
then laying it on about *Life on Earth*
with a tale great-granny had fed her

while we drew pictures on blank distance
pink and white striped flower ...a pest...
Beth on her knees trying to grub it out
...it ran miles underground...
...they couldn't help loving it...

The petals flopped and stuck to our fingers;
we pulled out stems, felt them grow more wiry
close to the ground, and thought how roots
had hidden through storms and droughts
that drove humans to the moon.

Then we took off our helmets, breathed air
for the first time just as it was, unzipped
in the tug of our new gravity, lifted
and lowered our feet. We could dance now.
We think we'll go back there for good.

Tirra lirra by the river

Forgotten the rest of the words
just these over and over
losing hold of meaning.

The horse clopping, the sway of its shoulders
and these—no longer words
but a river.

I'll build a cell here. Rain, close the door,
outside in good weather, under the willows
get down to repeating,

Lord have mercy,
heavier than tirra-lirra
over and over.

Relating to fish

In that town, everyone gravitates to the waterside.
They lean over bridges, watch from piers, stare
through holes cut in walls and floors.

Pensioners forget their gardens; policemen
ease their shoulders; a teenager
unplugs his walkman; lines drop from faces,

They search for shapes that persist behind the ripples,
a tell-tale shadow sliding over gravel,
a pattern of bars. Wind lifts their hair.

Nights, some still come, walking softly without torches.
All they want's a fin, passing through
the reflection of harbour light.

They never talk about fish, except to tourists.
No fish-restaurant here. Try Edgemouth
five miles north, along the coast road. Why's

there none here? No-one's ever opened one.
All day fish swim in slowly from the sea
and hang there, close to piers and bridges.

Afterwards

The first day, Caliban runs
to all the places Prospero closed,
finds rowans still by the waterfall,
listens to blackbirds and running water.
He winds honeysuckle round his head,
climbs to the highest point, sits, does
absolutely nothing.
      The second day
he tears off his tunic and feels the wind.

The third it rains. He creeps inside the cave
and spreads in Prospero's favourite corner.
That afternoon he peels a hazel branch.

Sometimes a small plant grabs him.
He grinds dandelion—suddenly—
Orgrud. He gets his mouth round it—*orgrud*,
drops the root, plunges his hands in thyme,
—*Seee...la...?...M...me...ll...i...?*
goes back to grinding, slowly, scowling.

The tenth morning cloud piles in. He rushes
onto the cliffs and looks out. At the first drops
he lifts his wand, draws lightning on the black,
grunts pour from his mouth. He keeps on and on,
gets soaked. At last the sky clears, kittiwakes
loop meaninglessly across the waves.
He throws away the stick, explodes
into the only language he knows now
that Prospero taught him

till the phrases curdle, he hurls stones
like curses over the cliff, hears them hit
and bring others cascading down
while the gulls swerve and screech.

Sycorax

Bent by polio, she spent
her childhood listening
to the songs of old women
and their talk, watching
withered hands pick, chop, grind
foxglove, feverfew, heartsease.

Most people avoided her
and some threw stones at a thing
whose words spun at them sideways.
Dwarf, they shouted, *twisted brain,* turning away
before she wrenched her head round
and looked into them.

Later they gave her a shack
under yews on the edge of the village,
leaving her to make friends
with trees, the river, cats,
though after dark
they came to her with their aches.

Once she opened the door
to a man who stayed the night,

felt at home alone on an island,
nursing the first human who'd loved her,
thinking she'd always understood
why water threw itself at rock,
though sometimes here
the waves lay down and rested.

Later still

Without Prospero
he walks tall, enjoys his nakedness,
experiments with herbs—
which taste good, which give him dreams—
searches for his own words,

entices a cat, whose ancestors
jumped from a wrecked ship
and after many generations
it still wants a human—
lets it ride on his shoulder

to a valley with rocky walls
where he pushes back hazel,
stares down on bones
the wrong shape for sheep or deer,
a skeleton curled on its side.

He touches a shaky ankle
runs the rough tip of a first finger
up the calf-bone, over the hump of the knee,
the grey length of a thigh bone, over the pelvis
into a hollow where the stomach was,

gently rocks a vertebra; his hand lifts
and hovers, lands on her chin,
strokes the full curve of her forehead.
I could have come, I heard you calling
—and had to be one of them.

Once this island was all I wanted.
They've done for me.
You told stories about people and a place
you'd been glad to leave,
everything here was so beautiful.

Then I curled beside you and listened.
Now I look out at the sea,
talk to you in a foreign language.
I'll take this little animal in my canoe.
We're used to one another.

Miranda

Because you're the quiet one,
in a family where words
tear everything to pieces
I go looking for you;

because you never wear
quite the face I expect,
because you slide away
into birdsong;

because a dream spoke names,
neither of which was yours,
and we met next morning
under the pink horse-chestnut;

because Robin became my playmate,
we rode horses down gravel paths,
jousted on the back lawn,
sailed to Peru on the fir tree;

because I invented a language
and found it hard to remember,
because he faded and Catherine
became my daughter

you were born;
because your sister needed a sister,
your name has to do with wonder,
there was space for someone

not beautiful herself or even pretty,
podgy cheeks and dark eyes
a way of fingering a leaf
of standing and listening

no logic or common sense
can twist you out of my mind
where I go looking for you.

Mornings

And that was the first morning -
the kettle boiled and switched off,
plates got themselves washed,
cloud wasn't particularly low.

The second wasn't the same – not that
anything broke down, nothing fell
in pieces on the floor, the carpet
didn't get stained.

Something made funny little scrapes
between the floor and the vinyl, nothing
that could be tracked down,
not loud enough to be named.

No-one could say *this is definitely wrong,*
no-one smelt burning and yet
the air was the wrong colour,
difficult to move through.

Faces looked lumpy,
worn by currents,
there were no maps
to find a way into them.

Between

Thanks to Eavan Boland

Neither day or night in the garden,
a blur in which one fades
the other approaches,
when trees and houses step back
and darkness looks soft.

The motorway was an interim
focussed on whiz
carrying people I didn't know
to places I might never have heard of,
my destination still distant;

the services a lull—
coffee and over-sweet biscuits
in a haze of voices and crockery
when air stopped
shaking for a moment.

Then entering Kathleen's house
I see she's begun to shrink,
to lose weight,
but the present holds
in an exchange of smiles;

a lightness like the bat
here in her garden
tilting and turning an hour or so
out from the dark of the Leylandii
and back. Over and round us.

Waking

I put on the radio in the night.
It brought faraway stories,
nothing about her.

Now first light fingers in,
sun flashes off white paint.
A double image of the mirror

slowly sorts itself out
presenting only this room,
my eyes unable to find hers.

There's no dawn chorus
only a stillness with uncertain edges,
one collared dove repeating a message.

The day I saw a rabbit

I was papering with speedwell and bugloss,
imitating the ups and downs of a bank,
smoothing petals, running fingers along veins,
pressing two blues down onto size,
brushing clear varnish over.

I sang softly
with my back to the weight
of emptiness behind me,

my feet sank into the pile of a carpet
patterned with leaves that lay on grass
deep enough to brush my ankles
or floated on water rising against my knees.

I must have needed the wall behind me
because I saw your shoes,
polished, watery, higher than mine—
perhaps you'd found a stone to stand on, your feet
a little apart with waves sweeping round them.
I think you'd just said something.

I was beginning to feel a tiny, shuddering kind of cold
when I looked out of the window and saw this rabbit.

Yard, garden, village

This word is spoken inwardly, speak it out,
that is you should become aware of what is in you.
                    Meister Eckhart   Sermon for St. Dominic's day

i.m. Dorothy Nimmo

The Ribble's a pale yellow sheering edge,
pouring over Queen's rock. I watch
not thinking of her

or what she told me, just going home
to an old house, a yard with a retaining wall,
veined by water;

a garden with a view of roofs and chimneys,
nesting places for jackdaws,
runways for mice,

in the angle where Belle Hill
flows into Church Street
and cottages have clustered, drawing me

to live surrounded by stone;
yard, garden, village:
stable as a three legged stool.

This word is spoken

the way a torch ranges over shelves,
into the back of a cupboard,
explores the whole length of an attic,
cobwebs, a dusty passport, worm-eaten chairs,
half an apple, wizened, stuck to the bottom of a drawer,
silver fish under the sink.
The way an X-ray exposes her lungs.

Snowdrops are coming out, now
in their own time, later than other gardens,
hidden under cotoneaster and bay, not
where I'd choose to have them.

Planted elsewhere
they've died or refused to flower,
while these seeded themselves
through the shrubbery to the far side of the lawn,
always moving,
as old women said they would,
towards the sea.

Yesterday I looked from the road
down onto drifts
white flowers beside running water.
Wind blew, their heads leant downstream.

Already, I thought, somewhere miles away
seeds must have blown onto salty grass,
across a beach, let themselves
be sucked and swept out.

Black splodges on dry snow
—old sedum heads, with blotched pink stems—
greenhouse where it's just warm enough to sit,
well wrapped, after church first Sunday in Lent.
Wind stings like salt.

Go into your ground.

Dying sedums still hold up their umbels,
sunlight draws green from the stones,
the earth is held by frost, it's Lent.
I think of famished monks, a fishpond emptying,
boiled carp, wind through the cloisters, my fingers,
how thin glass is.

Go into your own ground and work there.

I strike ice with a spade,
the surface powders,
and at last—a dark crack, water seeps up,
under a solid half inch, enough air
for a hibernating frog to breathe.

This is a quiet time,
a time for things underground,
worms, centipedes, roots,
not exactly sleeping,
to wait.

I've seen plants die in frozen ground
for lack of water. A dry time.
Black ice in the yard. Take care not to slip.

Collared doves *croo*,
a hen blackbird takes cotoneaster berries,
blue tits grab sunflower seeds and now
a robin feeds one side, a sparrow the other.
quick, while the sun lasts.

At night they huddle behind dry leaves
in the thick of the beech hedge.

All those small birds
beaks in one another's feathers,
not moving, losing weight
from frames already so light
there's nothing to them.

Her cheeks have fallen in.

Sleep in all things....

She would not know time
        or creatures or images

She might see images in dreams—
        her lungs in the surgeon's hands,
When she woke she'd have moved on.

Four grey and white pigeons rise
and circle down towards the beck,
slates shine through bare sycamore.
Is this place real?

There you live

                —so light and silver
evoking weaver, cobbler, schoolmaster,
who left initials over the doors. If they came back
they'd find even walls have shifted, themselves
names in the churchyard.

There you live,
in the innermost of the soul

The village shines
not with the whiteness of bones,
but the quiet of pigeons circling under a grey sky.

Yesterday she was curled,
tiny, in the corner of the chair, talking

what at 3.00 am she'd wanted to do,
what she still thought of doing.

Today it comes to me
to write about the village:

church tower, pigeon perched
beside her on a crenellation;

pale faces below, flattened,
expressionless.

Does she hear clapping?
Step off. So easy—

mind softening into drugged sleep,
buzzard resting on a thermal,

Would the earth welcome her,
take her into itself?

There are no angels.

Yesterday, in the dark corner of the chair,
she teetered on an edge.

Go down gently

by the stairs.

Her daughter's just rung.
    And now
all I want is to stand in my yard,
this familiar, enclosed place,
and touch roughly shaped limestone

trace the flow of its laying down
in edges
wearing and wearing away
in a retaining wall,

the hill cut back and blocks laid
end to end in rippling courses,
that cover a raw edge the old way,
hold back soil and let rain through.

Soon it will be time
to go out, stand on the bridge,
watch stone walls tremble in the beck,
this year's pigeons circle.

Fields

I lie in the dark
and listen to you breathing.
Three windows look out on hayfields.

Cool air blows in, the catches rattle.
Blue-green grasses bend together,
a shiver runs over them.

You gather air in
pause on the crest of a wave,
and let it out relaxed and sure.

I feel my rib-cage expand,
as if a cave had opened. And closed.
It's hard for me, this rhythm of yours

like when your fingers slowly adjust
the tops of your socks, slide out from under the fold,
smooth them with one last pat.

I drove to the ferry. Roadworks.
Roadworks again and the pickup
that thought it owned the road.

I felt your warmth in the passenger seat,
knew you were locking your fingers, knew too
what anyone else might be saying.

Now, with the journey behind us
I see fields opening for us
where things will grow.

Wild garlic

Yesterday I came down the path beside the quarry,
opened the gate into the wood, pulled it to behind me.
It grated, because the track turns stony just there
where shadow begins and I looked for deer,
as I always do and never see any,
and wanted you,

though we've never come that way together;
I've never looked into that dark and smelt wild garlic,
while you made a joke you hoped leapt over borders
asking, *Was that—what I said—totally outrageous?*
and I'd refuse an answer, turning with pursed lips,
my eyes egging you on. Or you might tell me something
utterly convinced that whatever it was at that moment
was the absolute tip-top distillation of truth.
Not just there. Never on that path.

Sometimes

Sometimes she'd unzip a canvas purse,
stare in at an embryo in a frosty test-tube,
a blur insulated by layers of plastic
tucked in her left breast pocket.

She was intrigued by the way she'd forgotten
what she'd dreamt when someone put it into her hands,
was inclined to think it had something of her in it,
didn't expect it to grow.

Sometimes she saw an old woman with rolled up sleeves.
Her skin was pinky-brown, freckled, with stand-up grey hairs,
she carried a long silver spoon and murmured, *Open your legs
and let me implant it,*

but she'd wave her hand flabbily up and down, *Not now,*
as if letting it inside would change things too much.

Saying *Ah*

Her arm rested on mine
as we leant our elbows on a showcase
taking things in

a Roman doctor had a tongue depressor
a great thing of curved pinkish bone
he would look down a throat
to hold the tongue the same way
my father
used a flat piece of steel.

My tonsils all wrong.
He'd better cut them out
and graft them in lower down
where he'd like me to have balls,

get rid of a high-pitched voice
that havers on in foreign languages.
What was the Latin for *Ah?*

Air through the vocal chords, a softness, her voice
when we had the room to ourselves
        in a quiet
which returned that evening in the abbey
while a girls' choir chanted the *Magnificat.*

The upper cairn

Hilltop. The upper cairn
crumbly watchman to my left.

The sky leans forward, cumulo-stratus,
where white like handfuls of shed fleece
—picked from the fell, washed, carded,
combed out gently—
gives an uplift, a curl;

the far hills
no longer landscape,
obtrusions of the earth, long edges

under a sun smouldering to rest,
a dark shutter slowly sliding down over it;
—someone shutting a cast-iron stove,
staring into the embers; a little smoke rises
and is closed in—

A small north wind blows in the sound of traffic
and shakes the grasses. It's older than any of their species,
older than the rocks, the oldest thing here,
exploring my bones.

Exmouth

One bar released from a bar-code—
small black upright way out on the sands
that moves a few feet to the left, stops.

I rest my hands on the matt blue-green paint
of a cast-iron railing on top of the sea-wall,
send my mind out to a figure

that has to be a woman, newly retired,
expanding forward into the haze
where grey-green water mixes with cloud,

feeling light touch her from all sides
no longer crushed by bodies
processed by escalator.

The sky bends over her,
she's not aware of anyone watching,
only of herself flowing into the wind.

Beside the Wharfe

Sometimes a river seems to listen,
brown water, curled white feathers, a yellow leaf
turning and resting, as from time to time
something catches;

your voice running round person after person, their parents, life history,
my fingers turning over dead leaves, feeling how leathery they are,
how easily I can tear them apart
till I flash out at your next beginning

and then a long pause
· while we watch foam eddy under a sycamore
and detach itself, as if a counsellor
has slipped out of the room and left us together.